Black Achievement IN SCIENCE

Biology

MC
Mason Crest

Black
Achievement
IN SCIENCE

Biology

Chemistry

Computer Science

Engineering

Environmental Science

Inventors

Medicine

Physics

Space

Technology

Black
Achievement
IN SCIENCE

Biology

By DIANE BAILEY

Foreword by Malinda Gilmore and Mel Poulson,
National Organization for the Advancement of
Black Chemists and Chemical Engineers

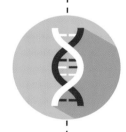

Mason Crest
450 Parkway Drive, Suite D
Broomall, PA 19008
www.masoncrest.com

© 2017 by Mason Crest, an imprint of National Highlights, Inc.

Printed and bound in the United States of America.

Series ISBN: 978-1-4222-3554-6
Hardback ISBN: 978-1-4222-3555-3
EBook ISBN: 978-1-4222-8322-6

First printing
1 3 5 7 9 8 6 4 2

Produced by Shoreline Publishing Group LLC
Santa Barbara, California
Editorial Director: James Buckley Jr.
Designer: Patty Kelley
Production: Sandy Gordon
www.shorelinepublishing.com

Cover photographs by Michael Zhang/Dreamstime.com.

Library of Congress Cataloging-in-Publication Data on file with the Publisher.

Contents

Key Icons to Look for

 Words to Understand: These words with their easy-to-understand definitions will increase the reader's understanding of the text, while building vocabulary skills.

 Research Projects: Readers are pointed toward areas of further inquiry connected to each chapter. Suggestions are provided for projects that encourage deeper research and analysis.

 Text-Dependent Questions: These questions send the reader back to the text for more careful attention to the evidence presented here.

 Series Glossary of Key Terms: This back-of-the-book glossary contains terminology used throughout this series. Words found here increase the reader's ability to read and comprehend higher-level books and articles in this field.

 Educational Videos: Readers can view videos by scanning our QR codes, providing them with additional educational content to supplement the text. Examples include news coverage, moments in history, speeches, iconic moments, and much more!

Science, Technology, Engineering and Mathematics (STEM) are vital to our future, the future of our country, the future of our regions, and the future of our children. STEM is everywhere and it shapes our everyday experiences. Science and technology have become the leading foundation of global development. Both subjects continue to improve the quality of life as new findings, inventions, and creations emerge from the basis of science. A career in a STEM discipline is a fantastic choice and one that should be explored by many.

In today's society, STEM is becoming more diverse and even internationalized. However, the shortage of African Americans and other minorities, including women, still exists. This series—***Black Achievement in Science***—reveals the numerous career choices and pathways that great African-American scientists, technologists,

By Malinda Gilmore, NOBCChE Executive Board Chair and Mel Poulson, NOBCChE Executive Board Vice-Chair

engineers, and mathematicians have pursued to become successful in a STEM discipline. The purpose of this series of books is to inspire, motivate, encourage, and educate people about the numerous career choices and pathways in STEM. We applaud the authors for sharing the experiences of our forefathers and foremothers and ultimately increasing the number of people of color in STEM and, more specifically, increasing the number of African Americans to pursue careers in STEM.

The personal experiences and accomplishments shared within are truly inspiring and gratifying. It is our hope that by reading about the lives and careers of these great scientists, technologists, engineers, and mathematicians, the reader might become inspired and totally committed to pursue a career in a STEM discipline and say to themselves, "If they were able to do it, then I am definitely able to do it, and this, too, can be me." Hopefully, the reader will realize that these great accomplishments didn't come easily. It was because of hard work, perseverance, and determination that these chosen individuals were so successful.

As Executive Board Members of The National Organization for the Professional Advancement of Black Chemists and Chemical Engineers (NOBCChE) we are excited about this series. For more than 40 years, NOBCChE has promoted the STEM fields and its mission is to build an eminent cadre of people of color in STEM. Our mission is in line with the overall purpose of this series and we are indeed committed to inspiring our youth to explore and contribute to our country's future in science, technology, engineering, and mathematics.

We encourage all readers to enjoy the series in its entirety and identify with a personal story that resonates well with you. Learn more about that person and their career pathway, and you can be just like them.

Four billion years ago, the Earth was not a friendly place. It was excruciatingly hot. The atmosphere was a hydrogen and helium soup that would have been toxic to any life forms. But slowly things began to change. The temperatures cooled slightly, allowing molten lava to harden into rocks that became the Earth's surface. Clouds formed. Rain started. Oxygen began to build up in the atmosphere. By about 3.8 billion years ago, there was enough oxygen to support the first tiny, one-celled organisms. They were simple and yet stunning—the kickoff to a process of evolution that has given rise to millions of species since then. They multiply, adapt, evolve, and die.

How does it all work? Why? It is the mission of biologists to study these questions and try to answer them. Above all, they are always asking more questions. Biologists peer into the most microscopic of organisms and gaze into the farthest reaches of the universe to understand the basic processes that form and sustain life. They investigate how life forms adapt to larger, outside forces, from climate change to war. The significance of what they find may not always be obvious, certainly not at first. But just as cells are the building blocks of life, the research findings of biologists are the building blocks of theories and knowledge that affect us in dramatic ways.

The study of biology affects every part of human life. Without advances in biology, we would know nothing of evolution. We would have no mechanisms to learn about and fight diseases. We would not understand how the food chain works, or why pollution can devastate entire ecosystems. Advances such as these have only come through years of work and research on the part of biologists and other scientists.

The relationships between all living things—plants, animals, and more—are the basis of biology.

Many of the fundamental principles of biology were being laid down in the eighteenth and nineteenth centuries. Scientists worked to categorize life forms based on traits they had in common. They began trying to understand some of the basic connections within and among organisms. Plants went on one side of the notebook and animals on the other. Botany, zoology, and later bacteriology were formed as distinct disciplines within the greater field of biology. Today, there are dozens of biology sub-fields. Some biologists still focus on a single species, while others might study a group of related organisms or the ecosystem they live in. Other biologists study a particular biological process, such as cell movement. Molecular biologists study the molecules that make up cells. Astrobiologists look into the possibility of life on other planets.

The reach of biological study expanded greatly in the twentieth century. There was a greater focus on experimentation and more effort not simply to observe different occurrences, but to explain how and why they happened. Notably, there were efforts to improve human lives using new discoveries in biology. For example, advances in the study of bacteria and viruses led to the development of antibiotics and vaccines. These would forever change the landscape of disease. Crippling epidemics of polio and influenza were eradicated by new medicines.

Another huge breakthrough came in the field of genetics. The idea that people could inherit traits had been around for centuries, but scientists did not know exactly what genes were, or how they affected a person's development. In 1953, the chemical structure of DNA (the genetic code within a person) was described. This was a revolutionary discovery, and let scientists take giant steps forward in genetics. They were able not only to describe why people looked the way they did, but also to use that information to fight deadly diseases such as cancer.

It is a basic part of a biologist's job description to study life and its processes. As they do, they recognize and celebrate the differences between species or members within a species. If nothing else, these differences pique our curiosity and spark debate. Why do fish swim and birds fly? How does climate change affect how trees grow? Can cells be manipulated to fight disease or carry medicine? Why are some people tall or short, or have black skin or white? Why are some people athletes or artists, and others are scholars or scientists?

In America, people of African descent have faced decades of discrimination. While not nearly as severe as it once was, this discrimination has left scars on our society. Despite the struggle—and perhaps because of it—extraordinary black individuals have emerged and left their mark. They have fought to educate themselves and to explore the things about which they were passionate.

The field of biology has been profoundly influenced by black scientists, not only in America but all over the world. The scientists featured in this book are examples of people who have worked to overcome racial discrimination, or who have built on the opportunities opened to them by those who came before.

Racial diversity is a latecomer to the sciences, but it is a vital part of it. Science occurs within a society, and race is part of society. The research topics biologists pursue may be influenced by race. The problems they find important—and the solutions they envision—also come as a result of their personal experiences and perceptions. Virtually everything we wonder about has some roots in biology. The natural world is a mysterious puzzle, and people of color are an integral piece of this puzzle. Answering questions—and asking new ones—is everyone's job. ●

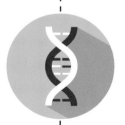

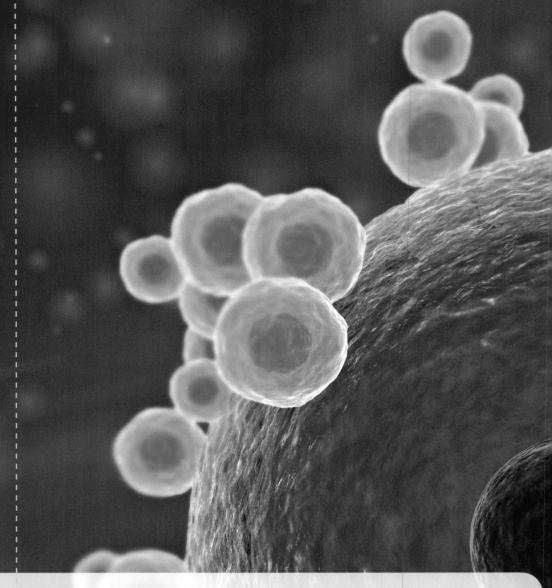

Words to Understand

embryo
an unborn animal or person in the process of development

holistic
involving all the parts of an organism, unable to be separated

invertebrate
an animal with no backbone

Chapter 1

Ernest Everett Just

Born:
1883

Died:
1941

Nationality:
American

Achievements:
Pioneering microbiologist, created new ways at looking at cell structure

"A house divided." Those are the words Scott Gilbert, a science historian, used to describe the field of cell biology in the early 1900s. They are also the same words Abraham Lincoln used to describe the United States during the Civil War. He was referring to the country's different views on slavery and the rights of black people. Even well after the Civil War ended, however, the United States was still a house divided by racism. In 1907, Ernest Everett Just was an African-American biologist first entering the field. He lived and worked in both of these divided houses. His scientific theories were sometimes controversial. Nonetheless, he worked to find answers and information all while struggling against the racism that pervaded the United States well after the Civil War.

In the early 1900s, few professional opportunities existed for African Americans. Just was born into a poor family in South Carolina in 1883. He had no early ambition to become a scientist. Instead, he went to school to learn practical skills such as bricklaying and carpentry. He was a good student, and eventually pursued more academic subjects. At a New Hampshire boarding school, and later Dartmouth College, Just became interested in science, particularly biology.

Howard University is one of the leading historically black colleges. It's located in Washington, D.C.

After his graduation, he went to teach at Howard University, a U.S. college for black students. Just had good timing. The college was working to expand, and Just was chosen to lead the new biology program. He wanted to teach, but he also wanted to pursue research. He found a mentor in Frank Lillie, who directed the Marine Biology Laboratory in Woods Hole, Massachusetts. Just began spending his summers there, doing research on the **embryos** of marine **invertebrates**.

Just was detail oriented and thorough in his research. He wrote dozens of papers that described different stages in embryo development. By the late 1920s he had earned an international reputation.

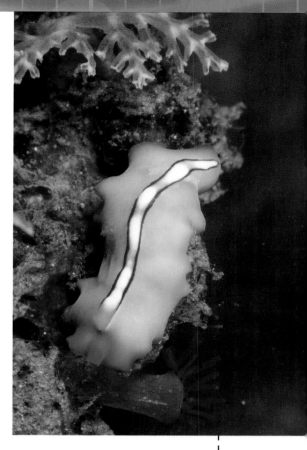

Just studied marine invertebrates, such as this blue flat worm from Indonesia.

Unfortunately, Just's scientific views did not always match up with those of his colleagues. Evidence for "hereditary material"—what we now call genes—had emerged in the mid-1800s. However, scientists were struggling to understand where genes were located, and what exactly they controlled. Some scientists believed that organisms developed strictly as a result of their genes, but others thought this approach was incomplete. Just was in the second cate-

gory. He supported a **holistic** viewpoint that an organism's development was more complex. It involved a combination of genetic and environmental factors. In other words, an organism's eventual outcome could not be known ahead of time. It would vary according to the events that happened along the way.

As he gained knowledge and experience, Just challenged the theories of other researchers. This gained him some enemies in the field. The racism in America during that time probably made these professional feuds worse. Even as he found himself at odds with his many of his fellow U.S. scientists, Just was earning respect and enthusiasm from European scientists who embraced his views.

He was eager to find intellectual collaborators and widened his sights to Europe. Rather than spending his summer research time at Woods Hole, Just traveled to Italy, Germany, and France, where he found colleagues who wanted to work with him. In 1938, Just decided to relocate permanently to France. While he was living there, he published an important book, *The Biology of the Cell Surface*. It synthesized the discoveries Just had made during his years of research. It also provided a philosophical approach to

To find the most freedom for his research, Just traveled to Europe, where he worked in the 1930s.

BLACK HERITAGE

USA
32

Biologist

Ernest E. Just

The U.S. Postal Service honored Just's contributions to science with this 1996 stamp.

science. The professional environment in Europe suited Just, but he was unable to stay. In 1940, World War II forced his return to the United States. Whether he could have reestablished a career in the United States will never be known. Just was sick with pancreatic cancer and died a year later.

Just's three decades of research were cut short by his untimely death, and the importance of his work faded. In the 1980s, however, a new biography about him revived interest in his career. Today, the holistic approaches that he supported in the 1930s find a modern parallel in systems biology. This approach to biology looks at how different biological systems interact and how they all contribute to an organism's development and life. "The egg cell . . . is a universe," wrote Just. "[Its processes] give us the story of all life from the first moment when somehow out of chaos came life and living." ●

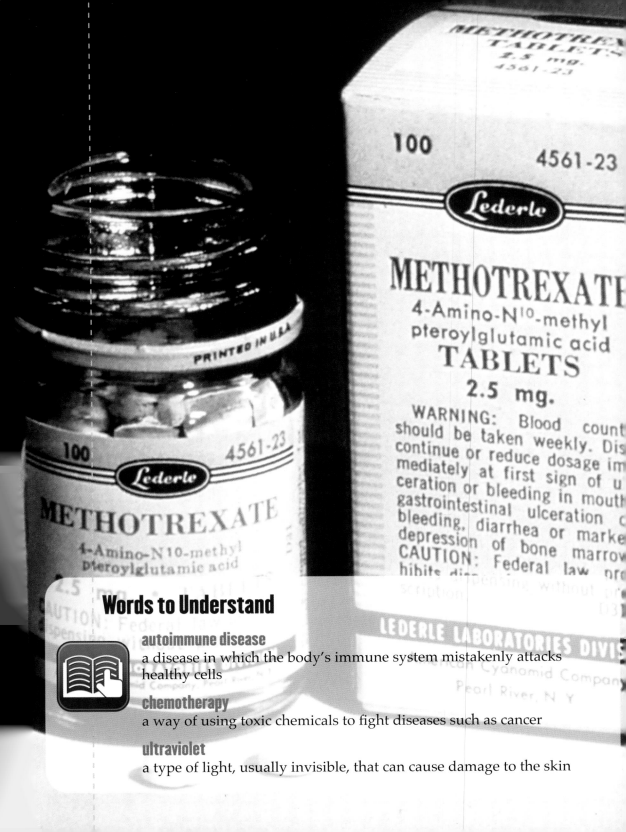

Words to Understand

autoimmune disease
a disease in which the body's immune system mistakenly attacks healthy cells

chemotherapy
a way of using toxic chemicals to fight diseases such as cancer

ultraviolet
a type of light, usually invisible, that can cause damage to the skin

Chapter 2

Jewel Plummer Cobb

Born:
1924

Nationality:
American

Achievements:
Found that methotrexate can treat skin cancer; investigated other skin diseases; later president of a major university

In the 1940s, Jewel Plummer Cobb had three strikes against her. She was black. She was a woman. And she was a scientist. In those days, such a combination rarely existed. Nonetheless, Cobb was determined to succeed.

She grew up the third in a line of medical professionals. Her father was a doctor and her grandfather was a pharmacist. The family discussed her father's work over dinner, and her Chicago home was filled with science books. Even with that background, Cobb did not decide to go into biology until she was in high school. In her sophomore year, she got her first chance to look through a microscope and was amazed by the things she was able to see. She decided to devote herself to science throughout high school and college and after earning a bachelor's degree in biology

Cobb worked at the National Cancer Institute in Washington, D.C., part of the National Institutes of Health.

in 1944, she went on to get a master's and then a doctoral degree in cell physiology in 1950.

That kind of education took most graduates into the medical field, but Cobb was different. She did not want to follow in her father's footsteps and be a doctor. Instead, she wanted to focus her efforts on research. She chose to join a research laboratory at the National Cancer Institute. There, she would study how cells operate and interact with other cells.

Cobb decided to concentrate on skin cells. She was particularly interested in the ones that held melanin, a brown or black pigment that gives skin its color. She wanted to know more about the connections between melanin and skin cancer. Some of her early work helped support the theory that exposure to ultraviolet rays from sunlight can lead to melanoma, a deadly type of skin cancer.

Cobb also studied various drugs used in **chemotherapy**, a standard way to fight cancer. One of her important discoveries concerned a drug called methotrexate. Her experiments showed the drug was effective in treating some types of skin cancer. It could also be used to fight breast cancer, lung cancer, and childhood leukemia. Today, methotrexate remains an important part of many chemotherapy routines. It is also used to treat **autoimmune diseases** such as psoriasis and rheumatoid arthritis.

Cobb's scientific contributions are still important in medicine today, but she also has influenced other areas. By the late 1960s, Cobb realized that although she loved science, she did not just want to do research. She was very interested in education and wanted to teach and be involved at the administrative level. As an administrator, Cobb thought she could have even more impact on students than she did as a professor. Gradually, she began devoting less

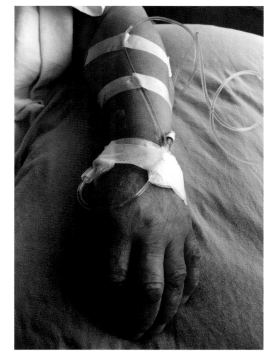

Cobb's research created new medicines used in chemotherapy.

time to research and more time to administrative duties. She took a closer look at how institutions actually functioned. An institution, after all, is similar to a giant cell. It has a lot of different parts. Those parts must interact and get along for the whole thing to function well. Cobb was well qualified to observe these processes. She found a lot that needed improvement, and one of those was the attention to minority students. At least the pigments in skin cells came in a variety of colors. It seemed like the students at universities mostly came in just one: white.

Cobb became the dean of Connecticut College in the early 1970s, and then later moved to Douglass College in New Jersey. In 1981, she went to California State University to become president at the Fullerton, California campus. At each job, Cobb worked to attract minority and women students to the sciences. There were a lot of hurdles. For one thing, she had to change perceptions on the part of administrators and faculty who were most-

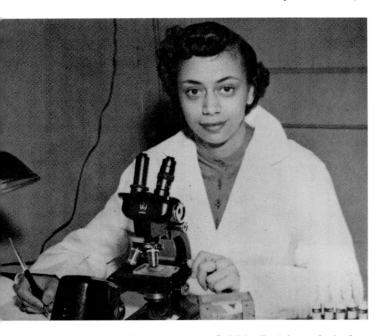

Research was Cobb's first love, but she later became a leading educator.

ly white. She also had to change the attitudes of the minority students themselves, who had often grown up believing they couldn't compete in the sciences.

Colleges had what Cobb called a "disastrous record" of recruiting African Americans to the sciences, but her efforts went a long way in changing that. She was rewarded for her decades of work in 1993, when the National Academy of Sciences gave her a Lifetime Achievement Award for her efforts in bringing minority youth to the sciences. ●

Cobb is one of only a handful of African-American women honored by the National Science Foundation.

Jewel Plummer Cobb, scientist and educator

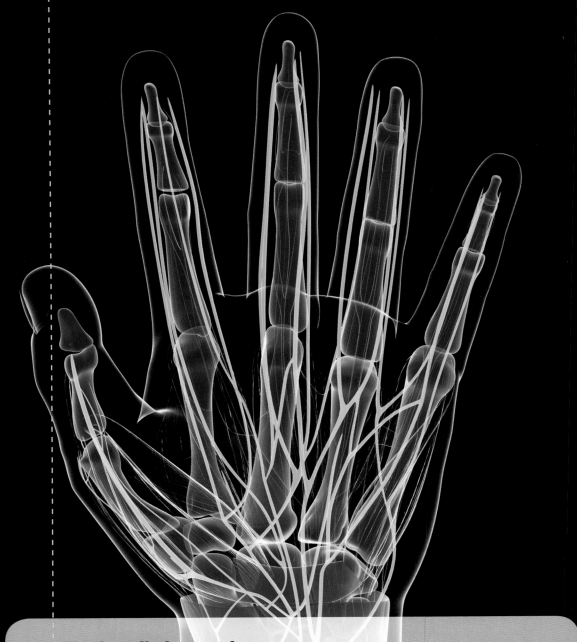

Words to Understand

filament
a long, thin fiber, like a thread

neurotransmitter
chemicals that send signals between nerve cells

Chapter 3

George Langford

Born:
1944

Nationality:
American

Achievements:
**Microbiologist who studies
how nerve cells pass
information through the body**

Put even the most everyday objects under a microscope and they look entirely different. When they are magnified hundreds of times or more they seem to change into something else. In high school, George Langford was transfixed by seeing how a microscope showed the underlying shapes and structures of objects. He also loved geometry and how it revealed the math that helped describe those shapes. He found that he had a knack for looking at a two-dimensional image and envisioning what it would look like in 3-D.

Langford grew up in rural North Carolina in the 1940s and 1950s. At that time, schools were still segregated between black and white students. Schools for black students had worse equipment and fewer supplies. There was only the most basic laboratory

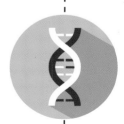

equipment at his school. Still, it was enough to get Langford interested in science. Also, because all of his teachers were black, he was able to see people of his own color working in science.

Langford decided to study biology at a small state university for African Americans. Again, the facilities were limited, and his opportunities were slim. None of his teachers were conducting research because black faculty members at small colleges could rarely get any money to do research. Still, Langford's mentors saw his potential. They encouraged him to finish his undergraduate degree and then continue his education at the graduate level. He went on to earn a master's and then a doctoral degree in cell biology. In particular, he wanted to study nerve and brain cells, which are some of the body's most complex.

In 1971, he began his postdoctoral research. He focused on cell motility (the movement of cells) as well as the nerve systems of invertebrate animals. Specifically, he studied how different parts of a cell move around and contribute to its overall function. Eventually he took a faculty position at Howard University.

In summers, he often did research at the Marine Biological Laboratory in Woods Hole, Massachusetts. In 1992, Langford was part of an international research team made a major discovery about how materials are transported within cells. In nerve cells, for example, **neurotransmitters** are packed up in small pouches called vesicles. Chemical energy then carries this cargo along **filaments** in the cell. The filaments act

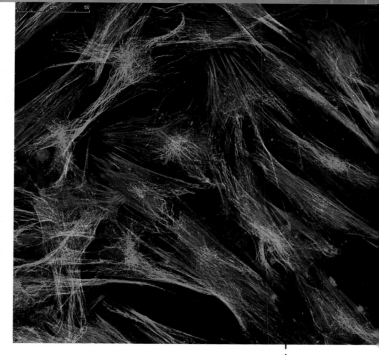

as roadways. Langford's team noticed there were things moving around in areas of the cell where there were no microtubules. What was happening? They believed that smaller filaments, known as actin, might be at work. To test their hypothesis, they injected a fluorescent dye that stained the actin and made it light up, revealing a "dual transport mechanism."

Scientists are able to examine tiny nerve cells after injecting them with dye.

Today, Langford continues his research at Syracuse University. He studies how brain cells contribute to learning and memory. Many people, especially as they get older, suffer from diseases that affect how these brain cells work. One of the best-known is Alzheimer's Disease. There are also other diseases that impair memory and brain function.

Throughout his career, Langford has worked to attract minority students. He tries to encourage them to pursue their education even when it is not easy. "You must maintain excitement for your science," he says. It is [your responsibility] to familiarize yourself with forms of racial discrimination and bias. You should develop strategies. Stay attuned to your goals, and try to understand the roadblocks." ●

George Langford

Words to Understand

impaired
prevented from working properly

phenomenon
a surprising and significant event, often a unique one

Chapter 4

Erich Jarvis

Born:
1965

Nationality:
American

Achievements:
Wildlife biologist looking for helpful links between elephant body systems and humans

Erich Jarvis could not understand what the elephant was saying. The problem was not that the elephant was mumbling, or that it spoke too quietly. The problem was that the elephant was speaking in Korean, and Jarvis does not understand Korean.

Jarvis was happy to listen to the elephant's remarks anyway. Even though he did not know what they meant, the fact that the elephant was talking at all meant something big to Jarvis. The elephant was showing evidence of "vocal learning." This is the ability of animals to voluntarily create, modify, and imitate sounds they have heard. Vocal learning is a rare characteristic. Humans take it for granted, but in fact only a handful of species can do it. Other species that use vocal learning include whales and dolphins, seals, bats, parrots, and hummingbirds.

Jarvis studies this **phenomenon**. As a professor of molecular neurobiology at Duke University in North Carolina, he investigates how neural pathways in the brain work. This helps demonstrate how the brain controls complex behaviors, such as speech. Jarvis is also working to understand how the genetic differences between humans and other primates affect the ability to speak. Why do humans talk but chimpanzees do not? By understanding how speech pathways operate in different species, he hopes to better understand the human brain. This, in turn, may lead to helping people who have an **impaired** ability to speak.

Jarvis did not always want to be a scientist. He grew up in New York City as the only child of two musicians. The performing arts were emphasized in his home, and Erich grew up dreaming of being a dancer. He attended a high school that focused on performing arts. He studied ballet and jazz, dancing six hours a day. At the end of his senior year, he was invited to audition for a respected dance company, the Alvin Ailey Dance Company.

At that point, Jarvis took a hard look at his future. He knew he wanted to do something that would have a positive impact on the world, and he knew he could

Dances such as this inspired Jarvis in his scientific work.

do that by being a dancer. However, he thought he could achieve even more by becoming a scientist to learn how the brain worked.

Jarvis had almost no background in science. He had only taken a few biology classes in high school. When he first entered college he was so behind that he had to take a lot of basic classes just to catch up. He graduated with degrees in math and biology from Hunter College in New York, and then went on to The Rockefeller University to finish his graduate work in 1995. Biology tapped into many of the same qualities he'd used as a dancer. "You become a scientist the moment you walk in the door of a laboratory," says Jarvis. "It doesn't start after you get your degree or your PhD or you've got your own job. It starts there."

Jarvis has discovered something interesting in his research. The parts of the brain that control speech are contained within other areas of the brain that control movement—including the ability to dance. "I'm actually coming full circle to bringing my scientific career and my former dance training together, because those two brain circuits seem to be related to each other," he says. "I hope in the future to discover what that relationship really is, and I think the answer's going to tell us how. This would be a natural, nice merging of art and science." ●

Erich Jarvis,
dancer-turned-scientist

Words to Understand

genome all the DNA in an organism, including all the genes

prostate part of the male reproductive system

Chapter 5

Rick Kittles

Born:
1976

Nationality:
American

Achievements:
Expert in genetics, examines roots of cancer; created database of African–American genetics history

Where are you from, originally? That seems like a simple question. When Rick Kittles was growing up, though, he did not have a simple answer. The white kids in Kittles' class could name some European country such as Germany or Scotland. But Kittles was black. The best answer he could give was, "Africa."

This answer was too vague. It bothered him. "I wanted to know where I came from," Kittles says. He was also curious about why people were different. Why did they have straight or curly hair? Why did some people get sick but others did not? Kittles was interested in all the "whys." In particular, he wanted to know how genetics contributed to these differences.

Kittles liked math and science, especially biology. He decided to study it in college,

and got a bachelor's degree in biology from the Rochester Institute of Technology in 1989. Then he went on to get a doctorate from George Washington University in 1998. For his doctoral work, he focused on population genetics, which looks at the genetic similarities of whole groups of people. He also studied biological anthropology, which is how biology influences human development. As a graduate student, Kittles began collecting, organizing, and analyzing genetic information from the African population. This has turned into his lifelong quest.

After receiving his PhD, Kittles went to Howard University, a traditionally black school. As an assistant professor of microbiology, Kittles helped set up the National Human **Genome** Center. Kittles and his colleagues collected DNA samples from hundreds of African Americans. They put together a database with all the information.

The amount of information in this database was staggering. A person has about 20,000 genes. They are grouped together in segments on strands of DNA. All put together, they make up a person's genome—

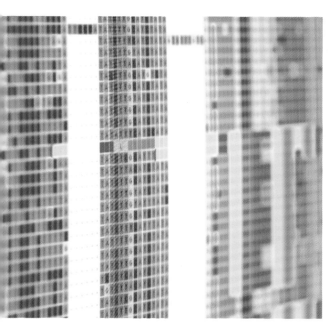

The information contained in DNA can now be read like a code.

Geneticists like Kittles often work in laboratories.

his or her complete genetic makeup. People share many of the same genes, but some are different. Also, the order in which they are arranged is a little different in each person. Finding out how they are laid out is called genome sequencing. Studying genes and their order is important for evolutionary biology. It helps explain why individuals or species look different, for example. It also helps determine how species may change over time (although environmental factors also play a role).

Scientists could use the information in the database to help them understand how genes affect diseases such as cancer. Over the years, Kittles has studied various types of cancer, including **prostate** cancer, breast cancer, and colon cancer. Currently, at the University of Arizona, he studies how genes make it more or less likely that African Americans will get certain types of cancer. He also looks at how their genes might play a part in treating the disease.

At first, Kittles' work in genome sequencing focused on how it related to disease. However, DNA holds a lot of other answers about people. Kittles realized that DNA profiles could be a way to help trace a person's ancestry, or genealogy. Genealogy research has been popular for years, but it is easier for white Americans. They often have written records in their families. They can trace their roots back a few hundred years. African Americans face a more

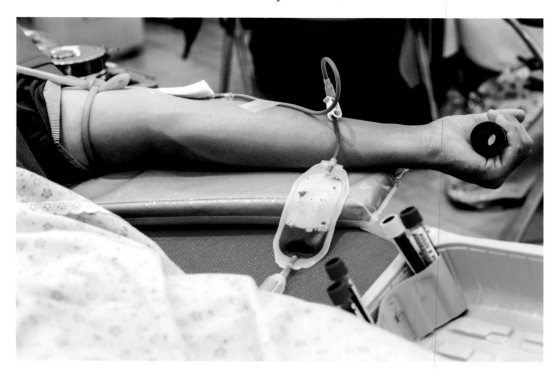

Geneticists can take blood samples from subjects and find out an enormous amount of information about a person.

difficult challenge. Many African Americans are descended from slaves, and their history was lost when they were forcibly brought to America. So, traditional methods of genealogy do not always work for African Americans.

Kittles set up a company called African Ancestry. People could send in a sample of saliva that contained DNA. Then Kittles' company would compare it to other samples in the database. Genetic markers can give clues to a person's lineage, including what specific areas of Africa their ancestors came from. "While the traditional historical documents might have been lost, the DNA is still there," Kittles says. "Within our bodies we have a record of the history of our families." ●

Kittles looked for a way to help African Americans connect to their families.

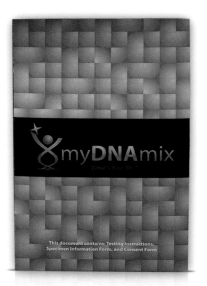

The website Kittles helped start connects people via DNA.

Words to Understand

gene expression
the way genes are activated in an organism to produce a particular characteristic

nocturnal
active at night

Outback
a large, remote desert covering much of Australia's interior

Chapter 6

Maydianne Andrade

Born:
1970

Nationality:
Canadian

Achievements:
Well-known expert on the Australian redback spider, as well as other arachnids; studies them to make connections about their behaviors

Watching horror movies is one of Maydianne Andrade's favorite activities—especially if they have spiders in them. She doesn't get scared, though. She has a couple thousand spiders hanging around in her lab at the University of Toronto in Ontario, Canada, so she is pretty used to them. It wasn't always that way. As a child, Andrade remembers watching TV with her two brothers in their home in Vancouver, British Columbia. A spider scurried across the floor. Andrade now knows it was completely harmless, but at the time she was terrified. The children climbed up on the couch to get away and to come up with a strategy to deal with it.

First, they trapped it under a bowl.

Next, the vacuum cleaner came out.

Looking back, it wasn't a great start for someone who went on to become an expert

in spiders. Andrade got over her fear of spiders, though, and now she is an evolutionary biologist who studies them. She specializes in the Australian redback spider. It is a poisonous, **nocturnal** species in the same family as the black widow. Instead of using a bowl and vacuum cleaner, Andrade now uses a headlamp and protective gloves to collect her samples.

Andrade planned to go to medical school, but after earning her bachelor's degree in 1992, she changed her mind. She wanted to do research, and she wanted to do it in the field. She liked the idea of being outside and observing things in their natural habitats. The work meant she was often hot, dirty, and lonely. After all, she had to go into the Australian **Outback** in the middle of the night to collect her spiders.

She says her love of research is similar to her love of playing basketball. Andrade is tired and sore after a game, but there's something about it that keeps bringing her back. Fieldwork is the same way. "You just have to be the kind of person, maybe a little obsessive, who is just so fascinated by what you're finding out that you're willing to go through all that pain," she says.

Andrade has to go where the spiders are and has made several trips to Australia's desolate Outback.

Redbacks are quite small but pack a powerful bite.

Andrade went on to get a master's degree in zoology in 1995, and a doctorate in neurobiology and behavior in 2000. From there she became a faculty member in the biology department at the University of Toronto.

Her research focus is on the redback spider, especially its unusual mating behavior. These spiders need to find a love connection on the first try, because the male won't get a second date. Instead, the female eats him *while* they're mating.

This behavior may seem a bit counter-intuitive. How does it work in with the idea that evolution depends on the "survival of the fittest"? Andrade thinks she understands. The real goal of evolution, she points out, is not the survival of any one individual. Instead, it's the reproduction

and survival of the whole species. That is exactly what the redback spiders do. The male Australian redbacks are small and weak compared to females. Only 20 percent of them ever get a chance at mating. The rest die while they're still looking for a female. When the male offers himself up as a snack for the mating female, the mating process continues for longer. This lets the male father more babies.

Andrade is now studying how the spider's mating patterns and environmental conditions work together. **Gene expression** is the way that genes show up in an organism. It is how we can observe a trait in an organism.

Environmental factors can play a big part in this process. Redback spiders have only a small window of time in which to reproduce, and they only get one shot. Because of this, their genes may be more likely to adapt to whatever the environment serves up. Other species, such as the Western black widow spider, live longer and mate more often. They are probably less likely to respond to short-term environmental changes. Currently, Andrade is

Andrade's study of the spiders is teaching her how they react to climate change.

Since spiders are nocturnal, Andrade, here with graduate student Emily MacLeod, works with her subjects in a darkened lab.

studying several different types of spiders to see how they compare. What she discovers may have an impact on people. The spiders she studies are poisonous to humans, for example. If certain types of spiders can reproduce easily, they may increase in number and pose more of a threat to humans.

Either way, Andrade just wants to find out more, even if it does not give scientists the answers they first expect. "I think it's important that we know as much as we possibly can about the natural world," she says. "The more we understand the better. There's sort of a beauty in knowledge, to watch and understand the intricacies of the world around us." ●

Maydianne Andrade, redback spider investigator

Words to Understand

poaching
illegally hunting animals

safari
a trip to observe animals in the wild

savannah
a large grassy area with few trees

Chapter 7

Malik Marjan

Born:
1965

Nationality:
Sudanese

Achievements:
Biologist founded wildlife society to track animals in Sudan, including migration patterns in response to ongoing civil war

For 22 years from 1983 to 2005, a civil war gripped the African country of Sudan. It was one of the world's deadliest conflicts. Two million people died from fighting, hunger, and disease. Millions more fled the country, desperate to escape the violence and poverty.

Malik Marjan grew up in this environment. It took a toll on his family, but Marjan worked to get through it. He got his bachelor's degree in 1993 from the University of Juba in Sudan. After that he went to the United Kingdom to pursue his master's degree in conservation biology.

Compared to his life in Sudan, things were easy in the United Kingdom. But Marjan did not want an easy life. He wanted to go home, where he could make a difference in his chosen field. The physical dangers fac-

ing him in Sudan were very real. There were armed rebels. There were land mines. What Marjan wanted to know was, were there animals?

Africa is home to some of the world's most varied and impressive wildlife. Elephants, giraffes, wildebeest, antelopes and gazelles live on the African **savannahs** that stretch through much of eastern Africa. Their migrations are amazing. Herds of thousands of animals trek across the savannahs in their annual search for water.

Hundreds of thousands of wildebeests cross the African savannah during their migration in search of water.

The shoebill bird, found in Sudan, comes by its name quite obviously.

But the war in Sudan had devastated the country. People were dead and cities were in ruins. It seemed impossible that the animals had not suffered as well. Pilots who brought food and medicine to Sudan in the 1990s had a bird's-eye view of the area. What they saw was not encouraging. The wildlife seemed to be gone.

Marjan hoped they were wrong. In 1999, he returned to Sudan and formed the New Sudan Wildlife Society. His goal was to search for wildlife.

Africa is so vast that it is very difficult to find and accurately count all the animals. The best way to do it is from a plane. However, when Marjan returned there were no large organizations that had people, supplies, and planes to do aerial surveys. There was no money for such efforts. The war had brought everything to a halt. In fact, he was one of only about 10 people trying to track Sudan's wildlife. They went out in cars and on foot to try to count animals. They took photographs and videos. Little by little, they began putting together a bigger picture.

Marjan's work drew the attention and help of people from another organization, the Wildlife Conservation Society. With their help, Marjan and his team were able to

do aerial surveys to count the animals and observe where they went.

"People thought we were crazy," Marjan remembers. "They reckoned that the rebels had slaughtered most of the wild animals for [food] and money from the sale of elephant ivory and rhino horn. But we proved that was not true."

What they found was astounding. The wildlife was not dead. In fact, there were even more animals than Marjan had expected. He thought he would find about 800,000 antelope and gazelles. Instead, he counted closer to 1.3 mil-

Marjan was surprised to find more animals, such as this Thompson's gazelle, than he had anticipated.

The Sudan plated lizard is an example of the biodiversity of the region.

lion. The team also found 8,000 elephants, 8,900 buffalo, and 2,800 ostriches. The list went on: there were giraffes, hippos, crocodiles, hartebeest, and more.

The team also took notes on the conditions of the land, as well as human activities. For example, **poaching** is still a big problem throughout Africa. Habitats are being lost from activities such as oil exploration. These could have big effects on the survival of wildlife in the future.

In 2012, Marjan completed his doctoral work at the University of Massachusetts, specializing in wildlife migrations. He hopes to continue his investigations in Sudan as well as get tourists to visit on **safari**. "I am hopeful that our government can find ways to harmonize nature and development," he says. "The data we collect provides the best argument for doing so." ●

Words to Understand

exoplanet
a planet in a solar system other than ours

Aomawa Shields

Nationality:
American

Achievements:
**Astrobiologist who explores
life on other planets; advocate
of science for young
African–American women;
actor and TV host**

Most people have wondered if there is life on other planets. Aomawa Shields is not content to stop there. She wants to know, "How do we go about answering that question?" As an astrobiologist, Shields investigates where life is likely to exist on other planets in the universe.

Astrobiologists analyze a wide variety of data from extrasolar planets, or **exoplanets**, that are in different solar systems. They want to see if those planets have conditions that are similar to Earth. If they do, they might be able to support life as well. Shields works to find planets that look like promising candidates. She uses a technique called climate modeling.

Climate is one thing that affects the ability of a planet to be habitable, or to sustain life. Climate is determined by several factors.

One is how far away a planet is from the star it orbits (its sun). That dictates how much light and heat it receives. Another is the atmosphere of a planet. Gases in the air affect the amount of heat that is retained or lost. Some planets are located at just the right distance from their suns that the temperature could sustain life. They are in what's called the "Goldlilocks zone." (The term refers to the fairy tale where a girl finds things that are "just right" for her.)

Shields is intrigued by an idea called Snowball Earth. About 600 million to 800 million years ago, Earth was ex-

Earth and the Moon exist in a "Goldilocks zone" of perfect heat and distance from a star. Is this repeated elsewhere?

An artist's conception of a possible exoplanet system.

tremely cold and covered in ice. It would seem like nothing could have lived in such a frigid place. In fact, evidence shows the opposite. It seems this period actually helped the Earth's first complex animals to develop. Shields researches what conditions could cause other planets to have a similar snowball state.

To astrobiologists on Earth, other stars and planets only show up as tiny dots of light on a powerful telescope. However, the type of light they give out can tell astronomers a lot. For example, cooler stars put out more light at longer wavelengths. Ice and atmospheric gases tend to absorb that type of light (and the heat that comes with it). That means planets around those stars could be warmer, and more hospitable to life. Other factors go into the equation, as well. For example, the shape of a planet's orbit could cause big temperature changes. If it passes too close to its sun, it will

get too hot. Too far away, and it would be too cold. Either one could prevent life from starting or surviving.

Scientists have found almost 2,000 exoplanets, which is too many to study in depth. Shields helps determine which planets should be explored further. Basically, she's putting together a master list and saying, "Okay, these planets are most likely to succeed. Let's point the telescopes there."

Shields' journey to becoming an astrobiologist began when she was watching the movie *Space Camp* at age 12, and decided she wanted to be an astronaut. She has not gone into space (she still wants to), but she has studied it. In 1997, she earned a bachelor's degree from the Massachusetts Institute of Technology. Her next step was to go to graduate school, but Shields had barely started when another interest sidetracked her: She wanted to be an actress.

She moved to Los Angeles and pursued a career in film and theater. After several years, however, she went back to science. She took a job at the California Institute of Technology, working with NASA's Spitzer telescope. "I realized I missed astronomy. I didn't want to hear about discoveries on the TV news with everyone else—I wanted to be part of it," she says.

She enrolled in graduate school at the University of Washington. In 2014, she finished her doctoral degree in astronomy and astrobiology. Now she works at the University of California, Los Angeles, and for the Harvard-Smithsonian Center for Astrophysics. Shields is also interested in bringing science to the public, especially minority girls like

Shields want to connect young students here on Earth to the amazing things that can be discovered . . . out there.

herself. They traditionally have had few opportunities to get into science. In 2015, she launched a workshop program that combines astronomy with theater, writing, and art. The workshops are geared toward middle school girls of color. Shields hopes they will encourage minorities to pursue careers in astronomy and astrobiology. "If I can get girls to see a piece of themselves—their hair, a foot, their face and eyes, a finger—as connected to an exploding star, maybe that connection will stay with them as they start to encounter the inevitable challenges of a science career," she says. According to Shields, "There's no one way to be a scientist." ●

Aomawa Shields, astrobiologist

Careers in Biology

When did you first get interested in biology? Chances are, you weren't in school. Were you fascinated by the animals living on a farm? Did you wonder about the trees growing in your backyard? Perhaps you wanted to know why a cold made you sniffle, or why you got goose bumps when you went outside in the winter, or why your sister likes spinach but you hate it.

For George Langford, it was the first amazing look through a microscope. For Rick Kittles, it was being curious about his roots. For Maydianne Andrade, it was getting over her fear of spiders. There is no single path that turns childhood curiosity into a career, and the study of life doesn't start or end in a lab. There are, however, some good steps to take to pursue a career in science.

Education is the foundation. Begin taking

classes as soon as possible. Some science is required for high school graduation, but don't stop at the minimum. Enroll in extra courses that involve biology in some way. Anatomy, physiology, or environmental science are some possibilities. Don't forget about other branches of science, either, such as chemistry or physics. All the sciences intersect at some point, and there are lots of careers that start with "bio." There are biochemistry, biophysics, biomechanics, and biomedical engineering. All of these combine biology with other branches of science.

In college, you might pursue an undergraduate degree in general biology. This will give you a broad base of knowledge. You might also choose to go for a more specialized degree. Zoology, botany, and microbiology are all different fields in biology. Some colleges require a general degree. Others allow students to take specialized courses from the start.

Of course, you do not have to decide everything before you ever get to college. However, it helps to have some idea about what you want to do. That helps you make better choices about what to study. In high school, talk to a career counselor. The counselor may be able to help you job shadow someone in the field. You can follow them around, watch what they do firsthand, and ask questions about their work. That can help you identify what things you find interesting and want to pursue. Several organizations offer internships for both high school and undergraduate college students, too.

Do some research to find out where biologists work. Some biologists work at universities, teaching classes and conducting research. Zoos, aquariums, and mu-

Connecting animals of all species can be a part of a biologist's job.

seums also hire biologists. Biologists work for several agencies. These include the National Park Service, the Fish and Wildlife Service, and the Environmental Protection Agency. These biologists might study an area to help protect an endangered species. They could also learn about how humans are affecting other animals or the environment.

In 2013, only seven percent of the bachelor's degrees in biology in the United States went to African Americans. Part of the problem is historical. For decades African Americans have struggled against prejudice from a largely white scientific community. Fortunately, there have been efforts in recent years to attract African Americans to jobs in science, engineering, and technology. Biologists know that diverse ecosystems are the healthiest, especially when nature throws curveballs. A complex web of creatures and connections has more chances to survive. Life thrives on diversity. So should the people who study it. ●

More ideas to pursue about careers in biology

Text-Dependent Questions

1. What are two fields that had great progress because of advances in biology during the twentieth century?

2. What types of organisms did Ernest Just study?

3. What is melanin, and what does it do?

4. What are two types of filaments that move material within cells?

5. Why is genome sequencing an important element in medical research?

6. What are three species that exhibit vocal learning behavior?

7. Why does the Australian redback spider allow himself to be eaten during the mating process?

8. Why do animals in the African savannah migrate?

9. What is the Goldilocks zone?

Suggested Research Projects

1. Cancer affects all kinds of people, but not always in the same way. Choose three or four different types of cancer and find out how frequently they occur in people of different races.

2. Staining cells with dyes and pigments often makes them more visible through a microscope. Research some of the ways biologists use stains to observe cells and their movement.

3. Research the field of personal genome sequencing. Find out some of the advantages and disadvantages it could have on health care.

4. Find diagrams of the brains of several different species, such as humans, chimpanzees, elephants, or parrots. Discover what areas are larger or more dominant in each.

5. Migrations happen all over the world. Choose a species and determine its migrating pattern. When does it move, and how far?

6. On Earth, all life forms require water. Elsewhere in the universe, life could have evolved differently. Find out some of the possibilities for alternative life forms that scientists are considering.

Find Out More

Websites

www.biologycorner.com/worksheets/articles/
From cell structure to genetics to ecosystems, this site contains a number of articles on current biological subjects.

www.biography.com/people/groups/famous-black-scientists
Check out this site for information on more famous African-American scientists.

Books

Barry, Joyce Thornton. *Painless Life Science*. Hauppauge, NY: Barron's, 2009.

Greenfield, Susan. *Inside the Body: Fantastic Images from Beneath the Skin*. Toronto: Firefly Books, 2007.

Miller, Dean. *Great Scientists: Botanists and Zoologists*. New York: Cavendish Square, 2014.

Series Glossary of Key Terms

botany the study of plant biology

electron a negatively charged particle in an atom

genome all the DNA in an organism, including all the genes

nanometer a measurement of length that is one-billionth of a meter

nanotechnology manipulation of matter on an atomic or molecular scale

patent a set of exclusive rights granted to an inventor for a limited period of time in exchange for detailed public disclosure of an invention

periodic table the arrangement of all the known elements into a table based on increasing atomic number

protein large molecules in the body responsible for the structure and function of all the tissues in an organism

quantum mechanics the scientific principles that describe how matter on a small scale (such as atoms and electrons) behaves

segregated separated, in this case by race

ultraviolet a type of light, usually invisible, that can cause damage to the skin

Index

Photo credits

About the Author

Diane Bailey has written about 50 nonfiction books for kids and teens, on topics ranging from science to sports to celebrities. She also works as a freelance editor, helping authors who write novels for children and young adults. Diane has two sons and two dogs, and lives in Kansas.